Amazing Cherokee Writer
SEQUOYAH

Mary Dodson Wade

Enslow Elementary

an imprint of

Enslow Publishers, Inc.

40 Industrial Road
Box 398
Berkeley Heights, NJ 07922
USA

http://www.enslow.com

AMAZING AMERICANS

Enslow Elementary, an imprint of Enslow Publishers, Inc.
Enslow Elementary® is a registered trademark of Enslow Publishers, Inc.

Library of Congress Cataloging-in-Publication Data

Wade, Mary Dodson.
    Amazing Cherokee writer Sequoyah / Mary Dodson Wade.
      p. cm. — (Amazing Americans)
    Includes index.
    Summary: "Readers will find out about Sequoyah's life, and how he created the Cherokee alphabet in this entry-level biography"—Provided by publisher.
    ISBN-13: 978-0-7660-3285-9
    ISBN-10: 0-7660-3285-X
    1. Cherokee Indians—Biography—Juvenile literature. 2. Cherokee language—Writing—Juvenile literature. 3. Cherokee language—Alphabet—Juvenile literature. I. Title.
    E99.C5S38922 2008
    975.004'97557--dc22
                  2008024893

Printed in the United States of America

10 9 8 7 6 5 4 3 2 1

Illustration Credits: © Billy E. Barnes/Photo Edit, p. 19; Eon Images, p. 1; © 2008 Jupiterimages Corp., p. 11; Library of Congress, Prints and Photographs Division, p. 16; © Marilyn Angel Wynn/Nativestock, pp. 7, 12; Oklahoma State Capitol, p. 4; Research Division of the Oklahoma Historical Society, p. 8; The WOOLAROC MUSEUM, Bartlesville, OK, p. 15.

Cover Illustrations: Eon Images (Sequoyah); The WOOLAROC MUSEUM, Bartlesville, OK (Trail of Tears).

Cover Caption: This painting shows Sequoyah displaying his syllabary for the Cherokee language.

CONTENTS

Chapter 1

Growing Up

Sequoyah (Sah-KWA-yuh) was born around 1776 in Tennessee. He was a Cherokee Indian. As an adult, he did not know how to read or write. Sequoyah invented letters and symbols for Cherokee words. He changed the lives of his people forever.

◀ Sequoyah created a way for the Cherokee people to write.

Sequoyah grew up to become a silversmith. He wanted to sign the pieces he made. A friend showed Sequoyah how to write his name in English.

These buildings are near where people think Sequoyah was born. ▶

CHAPTER 2

Creating the Cherokee Syllabary

Sequoyah saw American soldiers looking at papers. There were marks on the papers that the soldiers could read. Sequoyah called these papers "talking leaves."

Sequoyah wanted to make talking leaves for Cherokee words. He began to write symbols on paper and pieces of wood. Soon he realized he could not think of enough marks for each word.

◀ This is the inside of Sequoyah's cabin in Oklahoma.

He moved to a cabin in the woods to work on his list of words. His fields became full of weeds. His wife became angry. One day she burned up all of his writing. Sequoyah started again.

Then he got an idea from a children's book in English. It used only 26 marks to make all the words. Sequoyah listened to Cherokees speak. This time he made a mark for each sound he heard. After 12 years he finished the syllabary. It was made up of 85 marks.

Sequoyah worked hard to create a written language for the Cherokee people. ▶

Cherokee Alphabet.

Ꭰ a	Ꭱ e	Ꭲ i	Ꭳ o	Ꭴ u	Ꭵ v
Ꭶ ga Ꭷ ka	Ꭸ ge	Ꭹ gi	Ꭺ go	Ꭻ gu	Ꭼ gv
Ꭽ ha	Ꭾ he	Ꭿ hi	Ꮀ ho	Ꮁ hu	Ꮂ hv
Ꮃ la	Ꮄ le	Ꮅ li	Ꮆ lo	Ꮇ lu	Ꮈ lv
Ꮉ ma	Ꮊ me	Ꮋ mi	Ꮌ mo	Ꮍ mu	
Ꮎ na Ꮏ hna Ꮐ nah	Ꮑ ne	Ꮒ ni	Ꮓ no	Ꮔ nu	Ꮕ nv
Ꮖ qua	Ꮗ que	Ꮘ qui	Ꮙ quo	Ꮚ quu	Ꮛ quv
Ꮜ sa Ꮝ s	Ꮞ se	Ꮟ si	Ꮠ so	Ꮡ su	Ꮢ sv
Ꮣ da Ꮤ ta	Ꮥ de Ꮦ te	Ꮧ di Ꮨ ti	Ꮩ do	Ꮪ du	Ꮫ dv
Ꮬ dla Ꮭ tla	Ꮮ tle	Ꮯ tli	Ꮰ tlo	Ꮱ tlu	Ꮲ tlv
Ꮳ tsa	Ꮴ tse	Ꮵ tsi	Ꮶ tso	Ꮷ tsu	Ꮸ tsv
Ꮹ wa	Ꮺ we	Ꮻ wi	Ꮼ wo	Ꮽ wu	Ꮾ wv
Ꮿ ya	Ᏸ ye	Ᏹ yi	Ᏺ yo	Ᏻ yu	Ᏼ yv

Sounds represented by Vowels.

a, as a in father, or short as a in rival
e, as a in hate, or short as e in met
i, as i in pique, or short as i in pit
o, as aw in law, or short as o in not
u, as oo in fool, or short as u in pull
v, as u in but, nasalized

Consonant Sounds

g nearly as in English, but approaching to k. d nearly as in English but approaching to t. h k l m n q s t w y, as in English. Syllables beginning with g except Ꭶ have sometimes the power of k. Ꭺ Ꮪ Ꮫ are sometimes sounded to, tu, tv and Syllables written with tl except Ꮮ sometimes vary to dl

CHAPTER 3

Teaching Others

Sequoyah showed the alphabet to leaders of his tribe. His daughter Ahyoka was able to read the words. At first the leaders thought he had used magic.

But the syllabary was simple. People could learn it in a week. Soon, nearly every Cherokee could read books and newspapers. The Cherokee leaders gave wise Sequoyah a medal.

◀ Sequoyah taught his daughter how to read.

When the United States wanted to take the Cherokee land, Sequoyah was chosen to go to Washington, D.C. The United States made the Cherokees move. Sequoyah helped his people move to Oklahoma.

Sequoyah went with the Cherokee people when ▶ they were forced to move to Oklahoma.

Chapter 4

Sequoyah's Legacy

Sequoyah was more than 70 years old when he went to Mexico to search for other Cherokees. He died there in 1843.

◀ Sequoyah would teach his syllabary to any Cherokee who wanted to learn it.

Sequoyah gave Cherokees the gift of reading and writing. His hard work helped preserve the Cherokee language forever.

Today, people still learn Sequoyah's syllabary. ▶

Something to Think About

Sequoyah's syllabary was easy to learn.

The marks stood for sounds. It works like this:

You want to tell your friend, "I see you."
You write, I C U

Can you think of other marks that stand
for words?

The giant sequoia trees are named or
Sequoyah.

Why do you think that is a good way to
honor him?

Sequoyah invented a way for Cherokees
to read.

What would you like to invent? Why?

20

TIMELINE

1770?—Born in a Cherokee village in Tennessee. Nobody knows the real year.

1815—Married Sally Waters and lived in Alabama

1821—Daughter Ahyoka helped show the syllabary to Cherokee leaders

1824—Moved his family west

1828—Went to Washington to try to help the Cherokees settle problems about their land

1829—Built a cabin in Sallisaw, Oklahoma

1843—Died in Mexico.

★ Words to Know

preserve—To keep.

silversmith—Someone who makes or fixes things made of silver.

soldiers—A person who serves in an army.

sounds—Something you hear.

syllabary—A list of marks that stand for sounds.

Learn More

Books

Dennis, Yvonne Wakim. *Sequoyah, 1770?–1843*. Mankato, MN: CapstonePress/Blue Earth Books, 2004.

Rumford, James. *Sequoyah: the Cherokee Man Who Gave his People Writing*. Boston: Houghton Mifflin Co., 2004.

Shaughnessy, Diane and Jack Carpenter. *Sequoyah, Inventor of the Cherokee Language*. New York: Power Kids Press, 1998.

Waxman, Laura Hamilton. *Sequoyah*. Minneapolis, MN: Lerner, 2004.

Internet Addresses

http://www.sequoyahmuseum.org/, Sequoyah Birthplace Museum, Vonore, TN 37885

Places to Visit

Cherokee National Museum
Tsa-La-Gi Cherokee Heritage Center
Tahlequah, OK 74465

Sequoyah Home Site, with log cabin home built in 1829.
State Route 101
Sallisaw, OK 74955

INDEX